Super Simple
Cultural Art

Super Simple
AMERican ARt

Fun and Easy Art from Around the World

Alex Kuskowski

Consulting Editor, Diane Craig, M.A./Reading Specialist

A Division of ABDO

ABDO
Publishing Company

visit us at www.abdopublishing.com

Published by ABDO Publishing Company, a division of ABDO, P.O. Box 398166, Minneapolis, Minnesota 55439. Copyright © 2012 by Abdo Consulting Group, Inc. International copyrights reserved in all countries. No part of this book may be reproduced in any form without written permission from the publisher. Super SandCastle™ is a trademark and logo of ABDO Publishing Company.

Printed in the United States of America, North Mankato, Minnesota
102011
012012

 PRINTED ON RECYCLED PAPER

Editor: Liz Salzmann
Content Developer: Nancy Tuminelly
Interior Design and Production: Oona Gaarder-Juntti, Mighty Media, Inc.
Cover Design: Kelsey Gullickson, Mighty Media, Inc.
Photo Credits: Shutterstock

The following manufacturers/names appearing in this book are trademarks:
Americana® Multi-Purpose™, Elmer's® Glue-All™, Glitter Glue™, Hershey's® Kisses®, Land O Lakes®, Lion Brand® Yarn, Paper Mate®, Pillsbury Creamy Supreme®, Scotch®, Scribbles®

Library of Congress Cataloging-in-Publication Data
Kuskowski, Alex.
 Super simple American art : fun and easy art from around the world / Alex Kuskowski.
    p. cm. -- (Super simple cultural art)
  ISBN 978-1-61783-211-6
  1. Handicraft--Juvenile literature. 2. United States--Civilization--Miscellanea--Juvenile literature. I. Title.
  TT160.K8735 2012
  745.5--dc23
                        2011024598

Super SandCastle™ books are created by a team of professional educators, reading specialists, and content developers around five essential components—phonemic awareness, phonics, vocabulary, text comprehension, and fluency—to assist young readers as they develop reading skills and strategies and increase their general knowledge. All books are written, reviewed, and leveled for guided reading, early reading intervention, and Accelerated Reader® programs for use in shared, guided, and independent reading and writing activities to support a balanced approach to literacy instruction.

TO ADULT HELPERS

Children can have a lot of fun learning about different cultures through arts and crafts. Be sure to supervise them as they work on the projects in this book. Let the kids do as much as possible on their own. But be ready to step in and help if necessary. Also, kids may be using glue, paint, markers, and clay. Make sure they protect their clothes and work surfaces.

Table of Contents

Abraham Lincoln

Abraham Lincoln was the 16th president of the United States. He was born in 1809 in a log cabin.

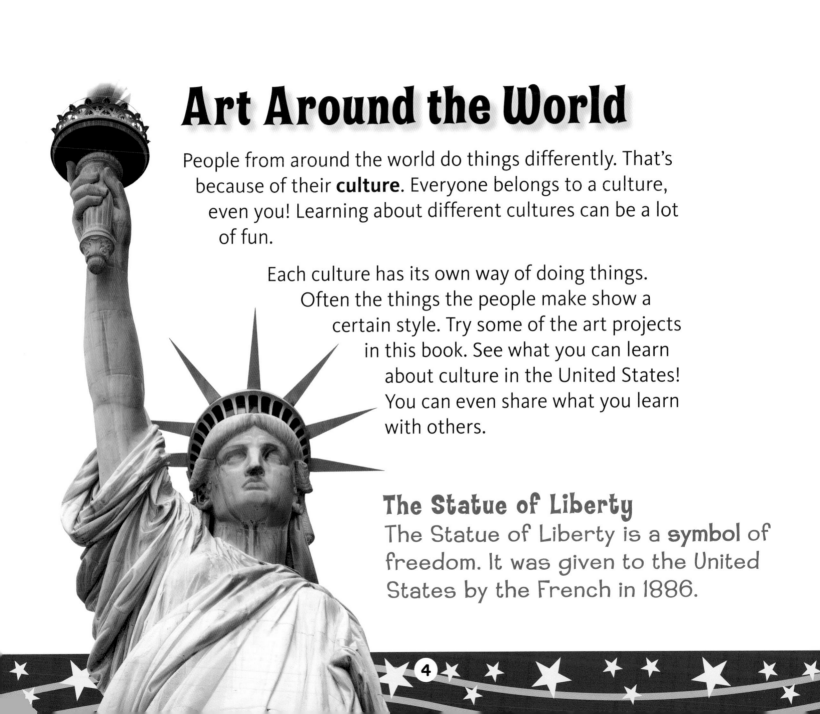

Art Around the World

People from around the world do things differently. That's because of their **culture**. Everyone belongs to a culture, even you! Learning about different cultures can be a lot of fun.

Each culture has its own way of doing things. Often the things the people make show a certain style. Try some of the art projects in this book. See what you can learn about culture in the United States! You can even share what you learn with others.

The Statue of Liberty

The Statue of Liberty is a **symbol** of freedom. It was given to the United States by the French in 1886.

Before You Start

Remember to treat other people and **cultures** with respect. Respect their art, **jewelry**, and clothes too. These things can have special meaning to people.

There are a few rules for doing art projects.

- **Permission**
  Make sure to ask permission to do a project. You might want to use things you find around the house. Ask first!

- **Safety**
  Get help from an adult when using something hot or sharp. Never use an oven by yourself.

Thanksgiving Turkey

Most Americans have a turkey dinner to celebrate Thanksgiving Day. The first Thanksgiving was held by the **Pilgrims** in 1621. They were thankful for having a good harvest.

Art in American Culture

The United States is made up of people from many different **cultures**. But one thing most Americans have in common is patriotism. They love America! There are many American patriotic **designs** and **traditions**.

The American Flag

The American flag is the most important **symbol** of the United States. The stripes stand for the original 13 colonies. There is a white star for each of the 50 states.

The Right to Vote

In the United States, voting is very important. It's one of the reasons the American Revolution was fought. The people wanted to choose their country's leaders.

Fourth of July, Independence Day

The Declaration of Independence was signed on July 4, 1776. It stated that America didn't want to be ruled by England anymore. Americans celebrate every July 4th with parades, picnics, and fireworks!

Materials

Here are some of the materials you'll need to get started.

construction paper

paper towel tubes

hole punch

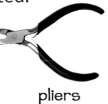
pliers

pencil

masking tape

glue

paint sealer

wire cutters

paintbrushes

cardboard

puffy paint

plastic lid

glitter

yellow tissue paper

drinking glass

chocolate frosting

glitter glue

yarn

tape

8

chenille stems

unpainted letters

pinecones

acrylic paint

toilet paper tube

screw eyes

pin backs

scissors

paper plates

brown pom-poms

black pom-poms

magnets

memory wire

pretzel sticks

letter beads

cereal squares

googly eyes

Hershey's Kiss

foam stars

red, white, and
blue beads

star-shaped
paper box

paper coffee
filters

empty
milk carton

self-adhesive
felt stars

9

Sweet & Salty Log Cabin

Abraham Lincoln lived in a log cabin made of real logs!

1. Wash the milk carton. Cut off the top of the milk carton. Then tape the edges together.

2. Spread frosting on one side of the carton. Cover it with pretzel sticks. Continue putting frosting and pretzel sticks on all sides. Cover the roof too. You may need to break pieces of pretzel to fit small spaces.

3. Put a little frosting on the bottom of a Hershey's Kiss. Stick it to the roof. This is the chimney.

4. Use small cereal squares to make windows and a door. Stick them on with frosting.

USA Magnets

Show your patriotism with these magnets!

1. Paint each letter a different color. Try using red, white, and blue. Don't forget to paint the sides. Let the paint dry. Add a second coat of paint. Let the second coat dry.

2. Paint a coat of sealer over each letter. Let the sealer dry.

3. Glue two or three magnets to the back of each letter. Let the glue dry.

4. Outline each letter with glitter glue. Let the glue dry completely.

Stars and Stripes Box

Fill these with candy for party favors!

WHAT YOU NEED
- star-shaped paper box
- pencil
- acrylic paint
- paintbrush
- self-adhesive felt star
- glitter glue

1. Take the lid off the box. Draw lines down the sides of the box. Try to space them evenly. Put the lid back on. Draw a star on the lid.

2. Paint every other stripe on the side of the box white. Paint the star white. Let it dry. Paint another coat of white. Let it dry.

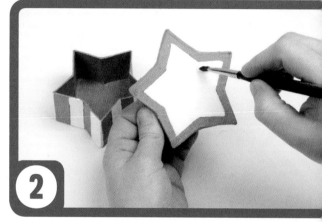

3. Paint the other stripes red. Let it dry. Paint another coat of red. Let it dry.

4. Paint the rest of the lid blue. Let it dry. Paint another coat of blue. Let it dry.

5. Remove the backing from the felt star. Press it in the center of the lid.

6. Outline the white star with blue glitter glue. Let it dry completely.

15

BLAZING ROCKET

It's a blast to make this 4th of July decoration!

1 Draw a line that winds around the paper towel tube. Make it about 1 inch (3 cm) from the **seam**. Start at one end and finish at the other end. Draw another line between the seam and the first line.

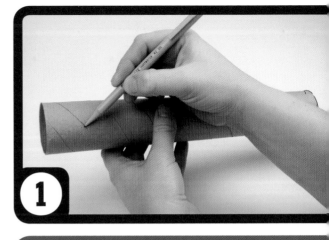

2 Paint each spiral on the tube a different color. Start with the white paint. Add a second coat if needed. Then paint the red and blue spirals. Let the paint dry between each coat.

3 Add a coat of paint sealer. Cover the tube completely. Let it dry.

4 Put the drinking glass upside down on the construction paper. Trace around the glass. Cut out the circle.

5 Cut from the edge of the circle to the center.

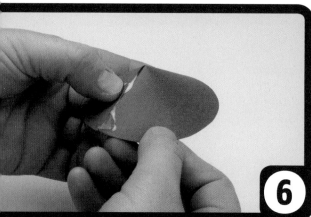

6 Overlap the edges of the cut to make a cone. Glue the top edge to the bottom edge. Let the glue dry.

7 Put glue around one top edge of the tube. Put the cone on the glue. Make sure it is centered on the tube. Hold it there until it sticks.

8. Turn the tube over. Add a little more glue. Let the glue dry.

9. Punch holes around the open end of the tube.

10. Wrap a chenille stem around the pencil. Slide it off the pencil. Put one end through a hole in the tube. Twist it to hold it in place. Repeat this step until all the holes are filled.

11. Decorate the cone and rocket with glitter glue.

12. Twist a screw eye into the tube. Put it near the bottom. Add a dab of glue around the screw. Let the glue dry. Tie a piece of yarn to the eye. Hang up your rocket. Blast off!

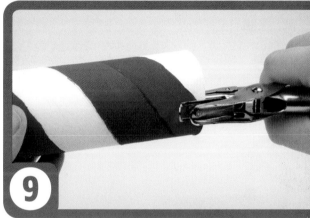

SWEET LIBERTY
HEADBAND & TORCH

You can be the Statue of Liberty!

WHAT YOU NEED
- 2 paper plates
- scissors
- ruler
- construction paper
- tape
- glue
- toilet paper tube
- plastic lid
- green acrylic paint
- paintbrush
- glitter
- yellow tissue paper

1. Cut out the centers of two paper plates. Cut 3 inches (8 cm) away from the edge. Cut a 3-inch (8 cm) gap in the edge of each plate.

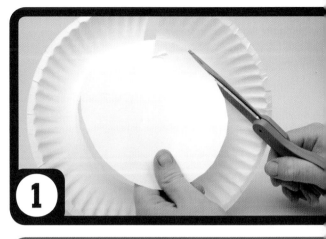

2. Cut six triangles out of construction paper. Make them 6 inches (15 cm) tall. Try to make them all the same size.

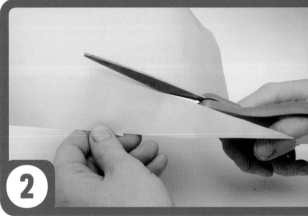

3. Tape the triangles to the bottom of one of the plates. Arrange them across from the gap.

4 Glue the other plate over the triangles. Make sure the gaps in the plates are lined up.

5 Cut a strip of construction paper. Make it 3 by 8 inches (8 by 20 cm). Cut a zigzag on one side. Try to make all the points the same size.

6 Glue the plastic lid to the end of the toilet paper tube. Let the glue dry.

7 Glue the construction paper strip around the lid. The zigzag should point up. Let the glue dry.

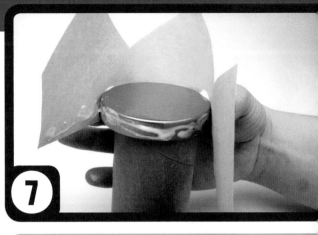

8 Paint the headband and torch green. Sprinkle on some glitter when the paint is wet. Let the paint dry.

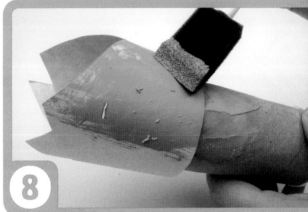

9 Crumple a sheet of yellow tissue paper. Make it look like a flame. Glue the tissue paper to the lid inside the torch.

PineCone TURKey

A cute decoration for the table at Thanksgiving dinner.

WHAT YOU NEED
- pinecone
- chenille stem
- colored construction paper
- scissors
- glue
- brown pom-pom
- googly eyes

1. Wrap the chenille stem around the pinecone. Press it between a row of scales.

2. Make three folds in each end of the stem. Pinch the folds together to make three toes on each foot. Bend the ends so the feet are flat.

3. Cut tail feathers out of construction paper. Glue the feathers to the flat end of the pinecone.

4. Cut a small beak out of yellow paper. Then cut a small **wattle** out of red paper. The wattle is shaped like a comma. Glue the beak and wattle to the brown pom-pom. Glue googly eyes above them.

5. Glue the pom-pom to the pointed end of the pinecone.

MEMORIAL DAY POPPY

The poppy is the official memorial flower for American war veterans.

1 Set the coffee filters on top of each other. Fold them in half. Then fold them in half again. Then fold them in half a third time. Round the corners off with a scissors.

2 Unfold the filters. Place them on a piece of cardboard. Dip the paintbrush in water and then in the red paint. Paint the filters. Put the filters on a paper towel to dry.

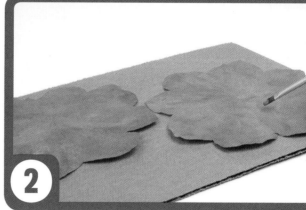

3 Put the filters back on top of each other. Turn them so the bumps are not lined up.

4 Poke a chenille stem through the center of the filters. Then poke the end back through the other way. Leave about ½ inch (1 cm) between the holes. Twist the end around the stem.

5 Gently pinch the middle of the filters near the stem. Wrap the other chenille stem around the area you pinched. Wrap the end several times. Then twist the two stems together to make one stem.

6 Crumple the filters. Then gently pull them open. Fluff out the flower.

7 Glue a black pom-pom in the center of the flower. Enjoy!

FUTURE VOTER

It's never to early to think about being a voter!

WHAT YOU NEED
- foam star
- pencil
- puffy paint
- glitter glue
- pin back
- glue
- memory wire
- wire cutters
- pliers
- red, white, and blue beads
- letter beads

29

Future Voter Pin

1 Write "Future Voter" in the middle of a foam star. Write lightly in pencil.

2 Paint over the letters with white puffy paint.

3 Decorate the star with glitter glue.

4 Glue the pin back to the back of the star. Let the glue dry.

Future Voter Bracelet

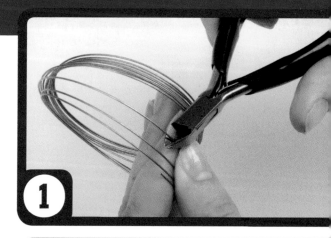

1 Cut a piece of memory wire. It should include three full circles. When **coiled**, the ends should be even with each other.

2 Use the pliers to make a **loop** at one end. Use the pliers to pinch the loop tight.

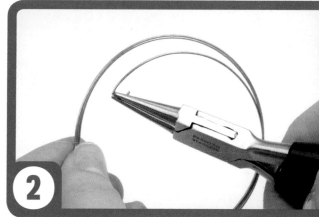

3 Put red, white, and blue beads on the wire. Add beads until the wire is about one-third full.

4 Spell "Future Voter" with letter beads. Put a bead between each letter. Add beads until the wire is full.

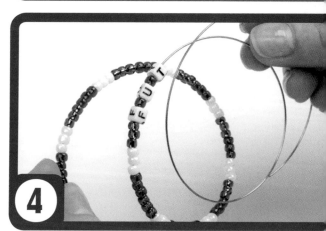

5 Repeat step 2 with the other end of the wire.

Conclusion

Did you learn about American **culture**? Did you have fun making these art projects? There are many ways to show patriotism! Try looking up more **information** about the United States!

Glossary

coil – to wind or twist into a ring or spiral.

culture – the ideas, traditions, art, and behaviors of a group of people.

design – a decorative pattern or arrangement.

information – the facts known about an event or subject.

jewelry – pretty things, such as rings, necklaces, and bracelets, that you wear for decoration.

loop – a circle made by a rope, string, or thread.

Pilgrims – a group of people who came from England to America in the 1600s.

seam – the line where two edges meet.

symbol – an object or picture that stands for or represents something.

tradition – a custom, practice, or belief passed from one generation to the next.

wattle – the flap of skin that hangs from the neck of some birds.